Contents

Any words appearing in the text in bold, **like this**, are explained in the Glossary.

What is water?

Water is a natural resource. It is mainly found in liquid form, but it can also be a solid or a gas. At room **temperature**, water is a clear liquid. Pure water has no taste or smell.

Water is made from two simpler substances, called hydrogen and oxygen, joined together. Each **molecule** of water contains one **atom** of oxygen linked to two atoms of hydrogen, so water is also known as H_2O ('H-two-O').

Water exists in three different forms in nature – liquid (water), solid (ice or snow) and gas (water vapour).

When is water liquid, solid or gas?

The state of water – solid, liquid or gas – depends on the temperature. If the temperature falls to 0 °C (32 °F), water turns to ice. If water is heated to 100 °C (212 °F), it will boil and become a gas. When water changes into a gas, the gas is called steam or water **vapour**. When steam cools down, it changes back into water again.

Why does ice float?

Ice floats on water because water behaves differently from most substances. Most liquid substances shrink a little as they cool down and become solid. These solid pieces are heavier than the liquid and so they sink. Water is different. Just before it freezes, it expands (grows a little bigger) and becomes lighter, so it floats. If water inside a pipe freezes, it can burst the pipe.

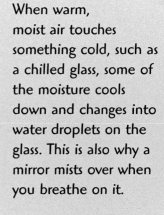

When warm, moist air touches something cold, such as a chilled glass, some of the moisture cools down and changes into water droplets on the glass. This is also why a mirror mists over when you breathe on it.

Ice cubes float on top of a drink because they are lighter than the drink.

What is water used for?

Water has many uses, including cooking, washing, heating and cooling. It also provides the power that makes some machines work.

Why is water used for washing?

Water is good for washing because it carries dirt away. It also **dissolves** some substances. Water and grease do not mix, but hot water can melt grease and carry it away. Soapy water removes greasy stains even better, because soap surrounds **particles** of grease and keeps them in the water.

How is water used for heating?

Many homes and workplaces are warmed by water. The water is heated in a tank called a boiler and then pumped through pipes to **radiators**. When each radiator fills up with hot water, it heats everything near it. The water then returns to the boiler, where it is heated up again.

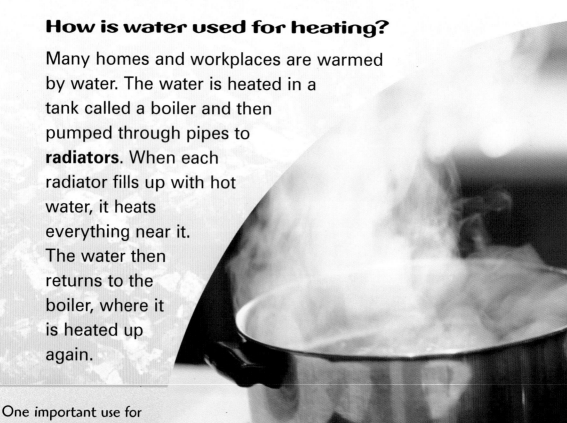

One important use for water *is* cooking.

How does water cool things?

If something hot is dipped in cold water, the heat flows out of it into the water. Blacksmiths cool red-hot horseshoes by dipping them in water. You use water to keep your body cool too. When you feel hot, glands in your skin produce a watery liquid called sweat. Heat from your body makes the liquid **evaporate**, leaving you feeling cooler.

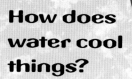

Firefighters use water to put out burning fires.

How is water used to grow crops?

Plants, including crops that provide the food we eat, need water to grow. Large areas of land are too dry to grow crops. Extra water is sometimes brought in through pipelines. Providing extra water for farmland like this is called irrigation.

Irrigation is essential to grow some crops in dry parts of the world.

How does water do work for us?

Moving water has energy, so it can make other things move too. If a wheel is dipped into flowing water, the water turns it. Adding paddles to the wheel 'catches' more water and so the wheel turns faster. People have used waterwheels for about 3000 years. They were mainly used to turn millstones to grind corn into flour to make bread.

Today, we use water to make electricity. Engineers use water rushing through a pipe to spin a turbine, a modern type of waterwheel. The spinning turbine drives a generator, a machine that makes electricity. Also, when water is heated to 100 °C (212 °F), it changes to steam. Steam takes up much more space than water. It pushes out in all directions. The force of the steam can also be used to spin a turbine and power a generator.

Did you know?

One way to make salt is to use the Sun's heat to dry out shallow pans of salty water. When the water evaporates, it leaves behind any salt it contains.

Waterwheels, like this one in Germany, have been used to power mills for centuries.

CASE STUDY:
The Space Shuttle spacesuit

It is very hard for an astronaut wearing a spacesuit to keep cool. When an astronaut gets hot and sweats, the sweat is trapped inside the airtight suit. It cannot carry heat away from the astronaut's body. Astronauts keep cool in a different way.

Inside their spacesuit, Space Shuttle astronauts wear a tight-fitting vest and pants with 100 metres (330 feet) of plastic tube sewn into it. Water is pumped through the tube. The cool water is warmed by the astronaut's body and carries the heat away. The water is then cooled down inside the suit's backpack and pumped around the astronaut's body again. The astronaut can adjust the **temperature** of the water to keep his or her body comfortable.

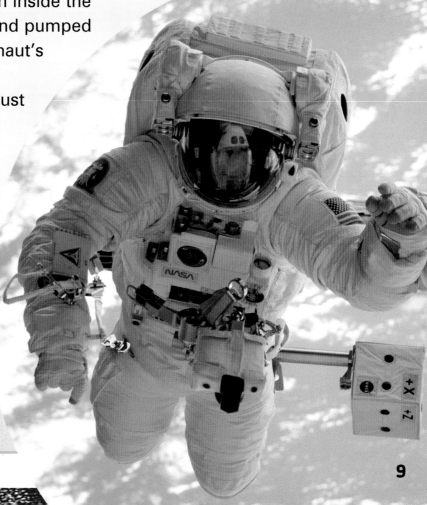

Space Shuttle astronauts wear a special suit that uses water to stop them from getting too hot.

9

Why is water important for life?

Water is essential for life. Life on Earth probably began in the sea. Millions of years later, some sea creatures crawled onto the land. They developed into new creatures, including dinosaurs. After millions more years, human beings developed. Although humans live on land, water is still very important. More than half the weight of your body is water.

How much water do we need?

People need about 2 litres, or about 8 cups, of water a day – though you need more on a hot day or if you are taking a lot of exercise. You lose water by sweating, going to the toilet and even when you breathe! Did you know that the lining of your lungs is moist? Every time you breathe out, some of the moisture is carried out with the air. All of this water has to be replaced. You get some water from drinks and some from food.

It is important to replace lost water to stay healthy.

How do living things use water?

Most plants and animals are made from tiny cells that contain water. The water fills the cells and helps them to keep their shape. If a plant is not watered enough, some of its cells become floppy and the plant wilts. Water also carries food and other substances around plants and animals to help their cells work properly.

Some animals can store extra water inside their body. Some people think camels store water in their humps. Actually, a camel's hump contains fat, which the camel lives on when food is scarce. It stores water in its blood. It can drink nearly 100 litres at a time. The water goes into its blood. The camel's body absorbs as much water as it needs until it finds another watering hole to drink from.

It is difficult for plants and animals to survive in places where there is little water.

Where is water found?

Water is found nearly everywhere on Earth. Almost three-quarters of the Earth's surface is covered with water. Almost all of it is seawater, which contains salt. Rivers, lakes, **glaciers** and the **polar ice caps** contain fresh water, without salt. This is water that has **evaporated** from the sea. When water evaporates from the sea, it leaves the salt behind. That is why rain is made from fresh water.

Where does all the rain go?

Some rain runs off the land into rivers and lakes. This is called surface water. Some rain sinks into the land and collects underground. Water that collects underground is called groundwater. Rock with lots of tiny holes in it soaks it up like a sponge. These water-filled rocks are called **aquifers**.

The Earth looks blue from space because of all the water in its oceans and **atmosphere**.

Did you know?

The Earth is the only planet known to have liquid water on its surface.

CASE STUDY:
Lake Mead, USA

Lake Mead is the USA's biggest reservoir. A reservoir is a human-made lake, for storing water. Lake Mead is 185 kilometres (115 miles) long and up to 16 kilometres (10 miles) wide. It was created in the 1930s when the Hoover Dam was built across the Colorado River on the Arizona-Nevada border. As the water trapped behind the dam rose, it formed Lake Mead.

Lake Mead not only supplies drinking water, it is also used to make electricity. Huge pipes carry water inside the dam, where it drives the generators that make the electricity. Enough water rushes through the generators to fill fifteen swimming pools every second. The electricity generated supplies 500,000 homes.

The Hoover Dam, a 221-metre (725-foot) high concrete wall, holds back the waters of the Colorado River to form Lake Mead.

How is water processed?

We can do lots of things to water. It can be **processed** in many different ways. One of the simplest ways is to heat it. Drinking water is heated for cooking food and making drinks such as tea and coffee. Boiling water kills any germs it may contain. Also, as we have seen, hot water can be used to carry energy from one place to another by pumping the water through pipes.

Another way to use water is to mix substances with it or to **dissolve** substances in it. Watercolour paints are made by mixing coloured materials, called pigments, with water. Sugar is often dissolved in drinks to make them taste sweeter.

This water was heated until it started to boil. Pure water boils at a **temperature** of 100 °C (212 °F).

How is water processed to make it safe?

Water is made safe to drink at water treatment plants. First, the tiny **particles** of mud and plants that make water cloudy are removed. This is done by adding chemicals that make the particles stick together, so that they sink. Smaller particles are removed by bubbling air through the water. The bubbles carry the particles to the surface, where they are skimmed off. Any remaining particles are taken out by letting the water flow through sand, to trap them. Any living **organisms** in the water are killed by adding a disinfectant, such as chlorine. In some countries, fluoride is also added to tap water, to reduce tooth decay.

Water in swimming pools has chlorine added to it, to make it safe for people to swim in.

Did you know?

Travellers and climbers in wild places sometimes have to drink water straight from rivers or lakes. They can make it safe to drink by adding **iodine** tablets to it or boiling it, to kill harmful organisms.

How does nature move water around?

The Sun's warmth **evaporates** water from the oceans, forming water **vapour**. The vapour rises until it reaches the cold air high above the ground, where it changes back into droplets of water. The water droplets form clouds in the sky. The water then falls back to Earth as rain or snow. The water runs down over the land back to the oceans. This continuous movement of water by nature is called the water cycle.

When water evaporates from the oceans, most of it stays in the air for about ten days before it falls back to Earth. Water that falls into the oceans stays there for much longer before it evaporates again – about 37,000 years!

Water is constantly moving from the surface of the Earth into the **atmosphere** and back again.

The water cycle

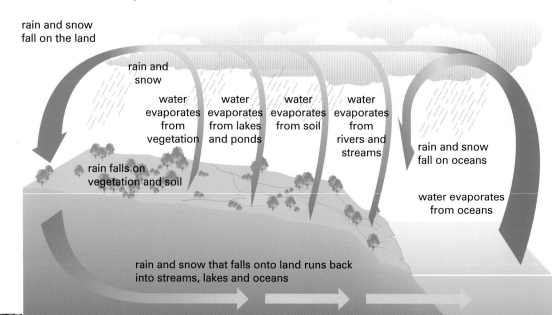

rain and snow fall on the land

rain and snow

water evaporates from vegetation

water evaporates from lakes and ponds

water evaporates from soil

water evaporates from rivers and streams

rain and snow fall on oceans

rain falls on vegetation and soil

water evaporates from oceans

rain and snow that falls onto land runs back into streams, lakes and oceans

How do plants move water?

Plants move an enormous amount of water from the land to the air. They take up water from the ground through their roots. It escapes into the air as water vapour through tiny holes in their leaves.

How do the oceans transport water?

Water flows through the oceans in currents, like rivers flowing through the sea. Near the poles, water cools down. Cold water is heavier than warm water, so it sinks. It flows towards the equator, where it rises and warms before flowing back to the poles. This journey takes about 1000 years.

Water flows downhill from mountains and hills to the sea.

Did you know?

Scientists have used toy ducks to study ocean currents! In 1992, thousands of rubber ducks fell off a ship in the Pacific Ocean. Currents carried them north. They were trapped in ice for five years, slowly drifting around Canada. They reached the Atlantic Ocean in the year 2000. Some were carried towards Europe while others drifted towards the US coast.

How do people transport water?

Water is so essential for life that it has always been transported from where it occurs in nature to wherever people live. In the ancient world, it was collected from rivers, lakes and wells in buckets, barrels, jars and bags.

Traditional methods of lifting water from rivers, like the one pictured here, are still in use today.

When people started living in towns and cities, they had to bring water in to meet their needs. They did it by building channels to carry water from nearby rivers and lakes. These artificial waterways were called aqueducts. Nearly 2000 years ago, 11 aqueducts brought 189 million litres (42 million gallons) of water into the city of Rome every day. It flowed into buildings through pipes made from lead.

Nowadays, cities can be built almost anywhere, because water can be supplied by pipelines. Some US cities have been built in deserts. One of these is Las Vegas. Most of its water is piped in from Lake Mead on the Colorado River (see case study on page 13). Some of its water comes from an **aquifer**.

How is water transported today?

Today, water is transported in lots of different ways. It is supplied to homes and businesses by pumping it through underground pipes. The pipes keep clean drinking water apart from dirty groundwater and waste water. Burying water pipes also stops the water from freezing in winter. In places where the water supply has broken down, water can be delivered to people in **tanker trucks**.

Fire trucks carry enough water in built-in tanks to deal with small fires, but they can also pump water up from underground water pipes or nearby rivers.

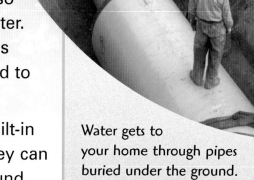

Water gets to your home through pipes buried under the ground.

Did you know?

People all over the world drink about 89 billion litres of bottled water a year. About 13 billion litres are drunk by Americans alone.

CASE STUDY:
Bombardier 415 firefighting plane

The Bombardier 415 is a firefighting plane. It has big tanks inside it to hold water. It is designed so that the tanks can be filled quickly and then used to drop the water onto a fire to help put it out.

The plane's tanks can hold more than 6000 litres of water. It can fill its tanks in only 12 seconds, by scooping up water from a lake or the sea while it skims across the surface, still flying. Then, as it flies over a fire, it can drop all the water in less than one second.

Firefighting planes are used in countries such as Canada, which have large forests and also lots of lakes. If there is a forest fire, the planes can fill up their tanks at a nearby lake and then 'bomb' the fire with water.

Firefighting planes are designed to carry water instead of passengers.

How can water affect the way we live?

Water has the power to affect our lives in bad ways as well as good. Storms, rain and high tides can cause floods. The most serious floods can destroy people's homes and crops. The sea can eat away at the land so much that cliffs collapse and buildings fall into the sea. Water may also be dangerous because it contains harmful substances such as germs.

The sea can wash away so much of a coast that buildings start falling into the sea.

How does water change the land?

Tides coming in and going out, and constant pounding of the waves on the land, washes the ground away in some places. This is called coastal erosion.

The US state of Missouri suffered serious flooding in 2000. A series of thunderstorms dropped more than 35 centimetres (14 inches) of rain in only 6 hours.

Storm surges

Big storms sometimes suck the sea upwards, like sucking water up a straw. Strong winds can then blow the heaped-up water against a coast. This is called a storm surge. In 1953, a storm surge in the North Sea raised the sea level by up to 4 metres (13 feet). It caused floods along the coasts of England and the Netherlands that killed more than 2300 people.

Hurricanes are very powerful storms, which can create large storm surges. One of the worst hurricanes to hit the USA was Hurricane Andrew in 1992. It produced a storm surge of more than 5 metres (16 feet) along part of the coast of Florida.

Sea-quakes

Earthquakes sometimes happen underneath the sea. When the seabed moves, it can make waves called tsunamis. These are small when they are far out at sea. They can cross an ocean at the speed of a jet-plane. In shallow water near land, they slow down and

Earthquakes under the sea can cause powerful waves that flood over low-lying land.

Did you know?

Tsunami is a Japanese word meaning harbour wave, because of the enormous damage they can cause there.

pile up higher. They can grow from less than 1 metre (3 feet) high at sea to 30 metres (100 feet) high near land. When a tsunami hits a coast, it sweeps away everything in front of it.

How might the sea change in future?

If the sea level all over the world were to change, the results could be disastrous. Many scientists believe that the Earth is getting warmer. If this causes the ice at the Earth's north and south poles to melt, the extra water would make the sea deeper everywhere. Towns and cities near coasts would be flooded. Low-lying islands could disappear altogether. The islands of Tuvalu in the Pacific Ocean are, at most, only 4 metres (13 feet) above sea level. They are already suffering from rising sea levels and could disappear altogether within 50 years.

Huge chunks of ice have been breaking off the ice caps at the Earth's poles and melting. The Larsen B ice shelf, containing 500 billion tonnes of ice, started breaking up in 2002.

CASE STUDY:
The Thames Barrier, London, UK

London has been flooded several times by water flowing in from the North Sea up the River Thames, the river that runs through the city. Today, London is protected from flooding by a barrier across the River Thames. Nine concrete islands, called piers, stand in a line across the river. There are steel gates between the piers. The gates are very strong and heavy. The four longest gates weigh more than 1500 tonnes each. They usually lie flat on the riverbed so that ships can pass through. If there is any risk of flooding, machines inside the piers swing the gates upright to close the river and keep the sea out.

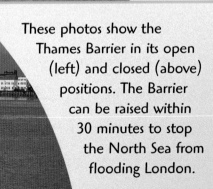

These photos show the Thames Barrier in its open (left) and closed (above) positions. The Barrier can be raised within 30 minutes to stop the North Sea from flooding London.

Why should we look after water?

Water is essential for life, so we need to make sure that we have enough clean water that is safe to drink. We also have to ensure that rivers, lakes and the sea remain clean enough for fish and other water creatures to live in, because they are an important source of food.

Is there enough water for everyone?

It may seem as though there is more than enough water for everyone, because most of the Earth is covered with water. However, most plants and animals on land depend on *fresh* water to survive. Only a tiny amount of the water on Earth is fresh water and most of that is frozen at the north and south poles.

The sea is an important source of food, so we must look after the oceans and keep them clean.

People in poor countries often find it difficult to get enough clean, fresh water. Even when there is enough water, it may be dangerous to drink. Poisoning is a serious problem in Bangladesh, because water in some wells where people collect drinking water contains a poison, called arsenic. It **dissolves** out of the rock the water trickles through on its way to the wells.

Wealthy countries can afford to provide their people with clean drinking water, but even wealthy countries cannot provide more water than nature supplies. The state of California, on the west coast of the USA, is one of the wealthiest parts of the world. Its population has grown from 16 million in the 1960s to 35 million today. Because of this, California is running out of fresh water. The state plans to make the extra fresh water it needs by taking the salt out of seawater. This is called desalting or desalination.

Seawater can be changed into fresh drinking water by taking the salt out of it. This desalination plant is in Kuwait.

How can we look after water?

We can look after, or conserve, water in a number of ways. We can try not to waste it, by taking as little as possible from nature. We can also try to stop water from becoming polluted with harmful substances such as oil and chemicals.

How can we use less water?

We use more water than we need to. We could use less water at home by using washing machines and dishwashers that are designed to use less water. We could take a lot less water from nature by repairing leaks in underground water pipes. In some places, more than half of the water sent out does not reach people because of leaks.

One easy way to save water is to turn off the tap while you brush your teeth.

How can we reduce pollution?

Pollution is reduced by cleaning dirty waste water from homes and businesses before it is released into rivers and the sea. Waste-water treatment plants do this important job. Gardeners and farmers can help by reducing the amounts of chemicals that they spray on the land, so that fewer chemicals are washed into rivers by rain. It is important to reduce **air pollution** too, because air pollution mixes with moisture in the air and enters the water cycle in rain.

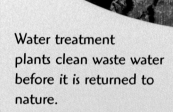

Water treatment plants clean waste water before it is returned to nature.

Did you know?

If you lived a few hundred years ago, you would probably use less than 20 litres of water a day for all your needs. We use a lot more water today. It is used for heating and in washing machines and dishwashers. People also wash themselves more often today than they did long ago. Someone living in the USA today uses up to 375 litres of water every day.

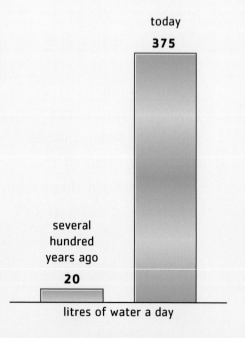

today

375

several hundred years ago

20

litres of water a day

Will water ever run out?

Water will not run out because it is not used up – it is constantly being **recycled** by nature. Drops of rain falling on us today might once have been drunk by a dinosaur! The water we use goes back into nature and it will be used again and again for millions of years to come.

However, we must continue to look after water. Water is useless to plants and animals unless it is clean. Many rivers and lakes that were once badly polluted are now much cleaner. In many countries, governments have passed laws to stop people and **industries** from polluting rivers.

Did you know?

In 1858, the River Thames, which flows through London, was so polluted that it smelt horrible. The smell was so bad that the British Parliament had to stop meeting. The river has been cleaned up since then. Today, the River Thames is so clean that fish, and even seals, are living in it again.

The same water has been circulating (going around) Earth for hundreds of millions of years.

Glossary

air pollution harmful or poisonous substances in the air

aquifer rock that holds water underground

atmosphere the gases that surround the Earth

atom small unit of matter

dissolve to mix a substance with water, so that the particles of the substance are spread evenly throughout the water. Salt and sugar can be dissolved in water, but sand cannot.

earthquake sudden movement or shaking of the ground

evaporate change from a liquid into vapour, or gas

glacier river of ice on a mountainside. Like rivers, glaciers flow, but very, very slowly.

ice cap a covering of ice that is always there, such as at the north and south poles

industries businesses that produce goods in large quantities

iodine chemical, used as an antiseptic (preventing the growth of bacteria, or germs)

molecule group of atoms linked together

organism animal or plant, from the tiniest germs to the biggest animals and trees

particle tiny piece

polar of the north and south poles

process to change a material by a series of actions or treatments

radiator device with hot water flowing through it, designed to heat a room

recycling using materials more than once

tanker truck truck that is designed to carry a large amount of water, oil or other liquid

temperature 'hotness' of a substance or object. Two commonly used temperature scales are Celsius (C) and Fahrenheit (F). On the Celsius scale, water freezes at 0 degrees and boils at 100 degrees. On the Fahrenheit scale, it freezes at 32 degrees and boils at 212 degrees.

vapour gas given off by a substance that is cooler than its boiling temperature. A dish of water left on a table slowly evaporates (turns to vapour), but when water is boiled, it changes to steam.

Find out more

Books

Awesome Facts About Tidal Waves, K. Petty (Franklin Watts, 2001)

Collins Gem: Weather, Storm Dunlop (Collins, 1999)

Dictionary of Weather, Storm Dunlop (Oxford Paperbacks, 2001)

Fantastic Facts: The Sea, Robin Kerrod (Southwater, 2000)

H₂O: A Biography of Water, Philip Ball (Phoenix Mass Market, 2000)

Seas and Oceans Facts and Lists, Phillip Clarke, Karen Tomlins and Luke Sargent (Usborne Books, 2003)

Water, Philip Ball (Phoenix Mass Market, 2000)

Websites

ww.epa.gov/safewater/kids/exper.html

Activities and experiments about water from the US Environmental Protection Agency.

www.groundwater.org/kc/kc.html

Information about water from The Groundwater Foundation.

www.waterinschools.com

Lots of resources and activities about water, from Thames Water in the UK.

Index